Secret letters from Spice: New York City Dog

Suzann Capra

Agora Books™
Ottawa, Canada

Secret letters from Spice: New York City Dog

© 2021 by Suzann Capra

All Rights Reserved. No part of this book may be reproduced, stored in a retrieval system, or transmitted in any form or by any means, electronic or mechanical, including photocopying, recording, or otherwise without the expressed written consent of The Agora Cosmopolitan.

Care has been taken to trace ownership / source of any academic or other reference materials contained in this text. The publisher will gratefully accept any information that will enable it to rectify any reference or credit in subsequent edition(s), of any incorrect or omitted reference or credit.

Agora Books
P.O. Box 24191
300 Eagleson Road
Kanata, Ontario K2M 2C3

Agora Books is a self-publishing agency for authors that was launched by The Agora Cosmopolitan which is a registered not-for-profit corporation.

ISBN 978-1-927538-52-4

Printed in Canada

Table of Contents

INTRODUCTION 5
Letter 1. A Life of Abuse. 7
Letter 2. A Life of Frustration 9
Letter 3. Surveying the Scene 11
Letter 4. Setting the Rules 13
Letter 5. I Am Superior 15
Letter 6. A New Awareness. 17
Letter 7. Another Dull Days. 19
Letter 8. No Respect for Me 21
Letter 9. Much to Complain About 23
Letter 10. I Am Psychic 25
Letter 11. Meet My Soulmate 27
Letter 12. Using My Telepathy 29
Letter 13. A Super Day 31
Letter 14. Taking Revenge 33
Letter 15. Using My Free Will 35
Letter 16. Home at Last 39
Letter 17. Second Day in the City 43
Letter 18. Getting Readjusted 47
Letter 19. Playing Matchmaker 51
Letter 20. Its Love Again 55

INTRODUCTION

Hi Pupper Parents,

It's me! Spice the City Dog communicating to you from the Doggy Planet with the power projecting ability that we all have. I left the Earth a while ago but before I left I asked my Auntie Evie to present my story to you. It's about my two week visit to the country. You will see that we puppers have an extraordinary inner life with our own unique goals, thoughts, and feeling, and that's why I want you to read my letters.

We pups are born on this earth plane to make sure that you are loved and you don't feel lonely. That is our purpose but if anyone hurts us then they will have to suffer a terrible fate either in this life or the next. We don't stay here for long because we live in a different biological time zone. We have no choice when we have to leave you but we can see you through our inner vision from the Doggy Planet

You can see us also when we visit you, but you have to use your inner vision instead of your physical vision. I always like to say that it is the truth that we puppers cannot see our own tails wagging but we can always feel our own tails wagging. We live in the energy space of feeling and that's where you can meet us.

Letter 1

A Life of Abuse

Dear Auntie Evie,

I am writing to you to let you know how horrible my life is. I don't get a break.

Every spring it's the same thing. The lady takes me and the two goofballs to the country. I don't like it. Why does she feel the need to leave the city? The country is a dull and boring place. There aren't any wonderful odours. Only trees, grass, bushes, and occasional cars to look at. I think I should report her for dog abuse. Not only that, but she leaves me alone in the house with the two morons who never have an original thought. They eat and sleep in the sun and use the wee wee pads and that's it. Granted, they do get up and bark if they hear a noise but then it's back to sleep. This is not any kind of companionship. Also, when the lady returns from wherever she went, she doesn't take me for a walk like she does in the city. Instead, she opens the front door and wants me to take myself for a walk in the screened-in area. What a nerve! Does she really think I enjoy this treatment? There are no great smells here and this routine continues every dull, boring day. I call this abuse and I am going to do something about this. I was thinking of starting a fund for myself called 'Help a Dog Escape from a Phony life'. Meantime, I'd better get a cookie before the two goofballs eat up everything in sight. Thanks for listening, Auntie Evie. I will write again tomorrow.

Letter 2

A Life of Frustration

Dear Auntie Evie,

Thank goodness we are corresponding. I really need to complain to someone and the lady doesn't listen to me. She's off in her own world. It makes me sick to see how lovingly she treats the two morons. She is always picking them up and cuddling them. I understand that she cannot do that with me because I am quite a heavy weight, but really, it's too disgusting and anyway, I don't like being cuddled by a lady. A man would be much better. I dream every day about the city streets and garbage. I long for their smell and other dogs to bark at, but mostly to feel my paws on the city pavement—*what joy*. All I experience here in the country is grass and dirt. No fun at all. Even the trees don't interest me 'cause there aren't any dogs to pee on them. It's impossible to communicate with the world when I'm here. The lady has her emails, but who do I have to communicate with? Only the two morons who eat everything in sight before I can get anything. The problem is there are too many rooms here. And the morons hide the biscuits all over, in all the rooms. The lady puts my cookies in the big, round, red bowl and we are supposed to share them, but that's not happening. The goofballs swipe my share and I can't keep guarding the bowl day and night. If the lady had a brain, she would give us separate bowls and teach them not to take my favourite cookies and hide them. In the city apartment there wasn't much room to hide anything and I could always find what I wanted. Well, Auntie Evie, I better start the search before I starve to death. The two morons are ruining my life. I will write again tomorrow.

Letter 3

Surveying the Scene

Dear Auntie Evie,

I have never known boredom like this. When I think back on my puppy hood, I recall my days being filled with anticipation, wondering who I would meet, what I would eat and how many people would think I was adorable. But now, I awake to the sound of nothing. Dead silence, except maybe for a few birds and the occasional car. I am almost tempted to start a game with the two morons to keep me occupied. I suppose I should call them by their names, but that would make it sound like I accept them in my life, which I don't. Maybe I will try. Maybe if I take a deep yawn and say their names quickly it won't be so painful. Here goes: 'Bubble' 'Amber'. Did it. Now I will breathe out the pain I feel in my mouth. Ugh. I'd better get a drink of water to wash-away the after taste.

Most people looking at my life would think it was idyllic, but from my viewpoint, it is not. I have a request to make, Auntie Evie. Would you please send a care package of dog urine from the city so I can sprinkle it around the trees? It would really help me feel like I was back home in the city. Thanks. I will keep two eyes out for it before the lady grabs it from the mailbox thinking it's for her. She has to learn that the world does not revolve around her. Well, I better grab a cookie if I can find one somewhere in the house. I think they want me to starve to death. I will write again tomorrow.

Letter 4

Setting the Rules

Dear Auntie Evie,

I'm sorry to tell you this and I am feeling a bit guilty, but I tried to bite Amber's nose. You see, it happened like this: I was sleeping on the lady's bed and having a very exciting dream and all of a sudden I felt something touch me and I went into attack mode. It was Amber. <u>Why</u> doesn't she stay on the floor in her dog bed, where she belongs? The lady's bed belongs to me and she should know that by now. She always brings out the worst in me. She needs to learn her place in this household. I am top dog but she will never get it. She's not good at problem solving- figuring things out. I tried to teach her the rules when the lady introduced us, but it's hopeless. I have to constantly growl at her. Another thing that is totally disgusting is that Amber is a farter. I sometimes call her Fart Face. She hasn't any manners. She doesn't even know how to do her business outside like a well-trained dog. She prefers to pee on wee wee pads. Wow, that rhymes—pee wee wee pee. I am so smart. Uh oh—Fart Face is watching me. I don't want her to know what I'm doing. She might decide to write letters to you, too. Although, to tell you the truth. I don't think she knows how to write and I'm not going to teach her. That's one of the only joys I have these days besides food. Which reminds me that I better check out the cookies the lady put in the bowl before Fart Face and Bubble eat everything. The only good thing about Amber is that she doesn't like to eat very much. Off on my food mission.

Will write tomorrow.

Letter 5

I Am Superior

Dear Auntie Evie,

I can't wait to tell you the good news. Bubble is in trouble. Oh, that rhymes. Bubble trouble! How clever I am! Anyway, it seems she was snoring all night and that really annoyed the lady. So now she is not allowed to sleep on the lady's bed. How happy that makes me. Pretty soon I will have the whole bed to myself, except for the lady, of course. Although I wish she would sleep somewhere else. She always disturbs me when she gets out of bed in the early morning to use the bathroom. I wish she would have more respect for me and wait till

I get up. After all, my middle name is ISIS, named after the great Egyptian Goddess and I deserve to be worshipped. But she doesn't understand. She is dim witted with no imagination. I say this because she bought three coats for the morons and me and they all look the same, except mine is bigger in size. I don't want to have the same coat as Amber and Bubble. We are not triplets. We are not even related and we hardly look alike. I feel humiliated to be dressed like those two morons. People say how cute we three look in our matching coats. It makes me sick and I am outraged to think she is doing this to me. She totally ignores my royalty, my roots, and my superiority. I never let her take a picture of me if they are included. I don't want to be seen with them. Doesn't she understand that they are beneath me in status? Only you understand, Auntie Evie. That's why I love you. You treat me like the Goddess I am. I will write tomorrow for sure. Maybe something exciting will happen, although I doubt it.

Letter 6

A New Awareness

Dear Auntie Evie,

I thought of a new name for Bubble. It's Bubble the Blimp. Don't you just love it? She looks like she is going to explode any minute and wouldn't that be nice. She's so fat that she can't climb up the new dog steps so I get to climb up and look out the front window whenever I want to without having to push her off. I am the watchdog here and I am on Dog Patrol most of the day. I let Amber do night patrol while I sleep on the lady's bed. Amber's hysterical high-pitched bark can scare anyone, except me, of course. I wonder if there are voice lessons for dogs?

Anyway, this morning I climbed the stairs and saw something move in front of house across the street. I totally focused, with tail out-stretched. I could feel my heart beating "Could it be?" I asked myself. Another dog across the street? Yes, yes it is! What bliss to actually have another dog right across the street? My tail went into wag motion. The dog was about my size and very nicely groomed. I could tell he thought he was hot stuff, 'cause when I started barking, he glanced my way but didn't bark back, a sure sign of conceit. Of course, he couldn't see me, but I felt that he thought that barking was beneath him. And he sashayed to his front door, totally ignoring me. Big mistake 'cause no living being ignores me. I am thinking of ways I can ignore him. Let me know if you have any suggestions, Auntie Evie. I will find out his name as soon as possible. I am going off Dog Patrol for now. I need to get a biscuit and ponder this new event. I will write tomorrow.

Letter 7

Another Dull Days

Dear Auntie Evie,

The lady has been acting very strange lately. She keeps dragging me over to the long glass hanging from the wall and forcing me to look at it. But then I just see the lady and a strange-looking dog next to her who I have never seen before. I am sure it's a dog because it looks like some ugly dogs I've seen in the city. I barked at it and put my nose to it but there was no doggy smell, just a cold feeling. I wonder about the lady's strange behavior and why she says these words: "You are a fat Chihuahua. Fat fat fat." What's that supposed to mean? The lady says this almost every day while looking at me. Doesn't she have better things to do with her time like making scrambled eggs with cheese for me to eat? Unfortunately, when that magic moment actually occurs, the lady forces me to share my portion with the Blimp and Fart Face. Not fair, not fair at all. I am bigger than they are and I deserve more. Actually, we share it four ways since the lady eats some of it, too. If I could just get rid of the Blimp and Fart Face, then I would only have to share the eggs with the lady. It's simple math. Oh, where is the passion in life? Certainly not in the country. The lady would cook special things for me when we lived in the city, but the country has made her lazy and she doesn't cook when we are here. This is not a place to bring a gourmet dog. Well, off to find a dull, boring biscuit. We will write again tomorrow.

Letter 8

No Respect for Me

Dear Auntie Evie,

I spent all morning hiding from the lady and I am all worn out. She got it into her head that it was time to take me for a pedicure but what she really meant was—it's time to visit the vet. What a horrible idea. She never comes up with anything original like going to the bakery and buying yummy cookies. Anyway, I'm stuck here under the bed so she can't get to me. Every time she tries, I growl and show my teeth. So much fun when I try to be fierce and look scary. Even Bubble the Blimp and Amber Fart Face don't know I am play acting and run away from me. I enjoy expressing myself in this way. Makes me feel powerful. After all, I am an alpha dominant female and everyone needs to respect that. I will have to stay under the bed until she gives up. The lady should be smart enough to keep water and biscuits under the bed in case of an emergency, such as "I'm hungry", or thirsty, but she is lacking in creative thinking and in having compassion for the needs of others. I often wonder why she adopted me. There were other people who admired me but my original mom thought the lady was the best qualified. They should have let me decide. I would have picked a man. I often wonder why the lady wanted me. Did she feel that I was her destiny? Was it chemistry on her part? It wasn't on mine, that's for sure, but I know how to play her, and that's what is important. Well, I guess I will have to stay under the bed until the afternoon when the vet's clinic closes. I will start leaving biscuits under the bed for the next emergency. I will write tomorrow if I survive this.

Letter 9

Much to Complain About

Dear Auntie Evie,

Another day, another disaster. What I want to know is who makes the rules around here? It's not me, I can tell you that. Everything would be different if it was up to me. I have many memories of a joyful puppyhood when I was in control and I made the rules. I decided which dog food and treats I would eat. I decided if I wanted to go for a walk or use the wee wee pads and where the wee wee pads should be placed. I also decided if I wanted to be picked up and cuddled. Now everything is taken for granted. The lady decides on the food, the walks and the cuddles these days and I don't like it. I seem to have lost all authority. Here is an example. The lady wanted to take a picture of me; but I demanded to be asked for permission, and the lady didn't do that, so I turned my back when she tried and she got a picture of my butt. Actually, I would like to see what my butt looks like. I never get to see it even when I chase my tail. Speaking of butts, I saw the dog that lives across the street. He is a real cutie with an adorable tail that stands up straight in a regal but self-important way. I will have to make friends with him, except he has a really conceited attitude. I guess he was raised that way. I blame it on his people. They are always hovering over him like he is a puppy. They are stifling his inner dog. I will have to change that. I am very talented that way. I will write again tomorrow. I need a biscuit ASAP. Letter writing really gives me an appetite.

Letter 10

I Am Psychic

Dear Auntie Evie,

Sometimes I wonder what life has to offer a great-looking dog like me. The lady has friends who visit and tell me what a lucky dog I am, but they don't have to live with her. Let me tell you that it's constant competition between the lady and me. I have to constantly whine until I get my way. I might as well create a band with me as the lead singer. I certainly have enough practice and can probably whine to a high C. But the lady doesn't care about my talents. Do you know that I can do wild back kicks and can run around in complete circles a dozen times with my tail held high? How many dogs can do that? The truth is, I know how to make people happy, which is something the lady will never learn to do. I could have been a super star. But the lady only thinks about her career — the height of selfishness. Who cares about her career? Doesn't she get it? I am the important one and the world needs to know it that. The two morons know it. They worship me, as they should and I didn't teach them to do that. They instinctively knew that. I wonder if the dog across the street knows that. I come from a very high lineage and am related to the ancient kings of England. I have papers to prove it. The lady is an ordinary commoner and hasn't any ancestry. Anyway, I will find out the name of the dog across the street. I wonder if he has any noble ancestry. I will find out. It's time for a biscuit. I will write tomorrow.

Letter 11

Meet My Soulmate

Dear Auntie Evie,

I found out his name. The lady and I went out walking this morning and I stopped in front of this house, which I have to say is not as nice as mine. Anyway, I barked continuously until his lady came to the front door and called him over. His name is Sir Wellington, not just Wellington, but *Sir* Wellington. He must have a noble ancestry, don't you think? He sounds very high-bred-and-born. Great match for me with my ancestry. I had better get a grooming and a pedicure. Anyway, he did not come to the door when called. That's being very disobedient.

Seems like very poor upbringing and I blame it on his lady. Maybe he needs to go to doggy pre-school and learn some manners. I have never had to go because I was always well mannered. I was born with a sense of right from wrong. I was a puppy that knew good from bad and was very respectful of people with their egotistical and narcissistic needs. I can read them like a book. I believe that I was born with psychic gifts. Some dogs are dull and boring like Amber and Bubble, but not me. I knew who I was and what I was capable of doing. I am a very talented young lady. Some dogs might be jealous of me, but I always make my demands known and people follow my lead, except, of course, for the lady. She actually thinks that she knows more than me. What a joke. I am in touch with divine powers and am very proud of it. What a mismatch we are. I should have demanded a better person to adopt me. But she appeared insecure and I thought I could change her and give her self-respect and feelings of worthiness like I have. Well, tomorrow, Auntie Evie, I am going to meet Sir Wellington face-to-face and butt-to-butt. I will fortify myself with biscuits and prepare for tomorrow.

Letter 12

Using My Telepathy

Dear Auntie Evie,

This morning I rolled around in the dirt outside to let the lady know that I needed a grooming. She doesn't have the brain capacity to figure that out for herself. So off we went to the groomer and now I am ready to meet Sir Wellington. I whined for a very long time when we returned just to get the lady to take me for a walk in front of Sir Wellington's house. She finally caught on and put on my harness and leash. The things I have to do to get through to her. The only problem was it started to rain and no well-bred dog walks in the rain. So disappointing. I had my hormones all worked up for this meeting and now I have to stay in with the two loser goofballs. I can only dream that the lady will occupy my time by cooking something mouthwatering delicious. That is the only substitute I will accept in place of my social life with Sir Wellington. I wonder what he is doing right now. Maybe he's dreaming of me, his soul mate. I will try to do dream telepathy and send him messages. When we finally meet in person, it will be electric with recognition. I had better get to work right now. Sending messages takes a lot of energy and I don't think the lady will cook for me. To tell the truth, the lady is an awful cook, except for her scrambled eggs with cheddar cheese and tomatoes. I think I should send the lady thought forms of eggs and cheese. Maybe I will be lucky but I doubt it. I hope it doesn't rain tomorrow so I can meet Sir Wellington. Talk tomorrow. Wish me luck.

Letter 13

A Super Day

Dear Auntie Evie,

You're not going to believe what happened this morning. Sir Wellington's lady brought him over for a visit. My dream came through. My lady greeted them at the door while I was in the kitchen guarding the biscuits. When I sniffed him out, I quickly hid the biscuits, did a few back kicks and rubbed my face on the small rug. I then did my Goddess walk and made my entrance. We made eye contact and he wagged his tail first. Oh, what joy to be in control and the object of desire. I sized him up and out of politeness, I proceeded to wag my tail. So we were wagging our tails at the same time. I knew at once that he knew that he had met his match. We walked toward each other at the same time. We then sniffed each other's faces and butts and finally we did back kicks and circled together. It was magic. We both felt the chemistry and ran to the wee wee pads and peed at the same time. Our meeting went better than if I had planned it. I guess I should have shared a biscuit with him but I have a great attachment to them and couldn't do it, but we drank water together. It was a day to truly be remembered, except, of course, for the two pinheads barking at Sir Wellington. It's so obvious that they don't have any class, and very embarrassing for me to be living in the same house with them but what choice do I have? Of course, I could move in with Sir Wellington but I don't think the lady would allow that. She needs me too much. I know she would crack up if it wasn't for me. I am her life's purpose. You will get to see him soon, Auntie Evie, because the lady took pictures of us together. We are going outside to run together. Will write tomorrow.

Letter 14

Taking Revenge

Dear Auntie Evie,

I think we are going home to the city. I awakened this morning after dreaming all night of Sir Wellington and I saw the lady putting together a pile of bags in the hall next to the cars' room. How could she do this to me right after I meet the love of my life? I must remain calm and survey this scene. I might be totally wrong but I am a psychic dog and I have my impressions, which are usually right. I can feel the goinghome energy. I am starting to feel addicted to it. Poor Sir Wellington, I don't want to break his heart. I can't leave now. What will he do without me? But the city awaits me. The great smells, the pavement, the hysteria. I love the city as much as I love Sir Wellington. If only I could be in two places at once. Wait a minute – what choice do I really have? I have to go where the lady goes. What a shocking recognition. I am starting to shake. The morons are watching me. I can't let them see how vulnerable I am. My reputation will be ruined. How difficult it is to be a symbol of self-control and power. I must face my fate. The lady is always ruining my life. I will have to put up a brave exterior and follow my destiny. Then again, maybe I could convince her to stay here longer. Let her know that I am not a total victim of her whims. But how do I do that? I feel that I haven't any free will. My head is beginning to spin inside. This is too much to contemplate. I will have to just sit here and watch and pretend to be ill. That always upsets the lady. She needs to have some pity for me. I will write tomorrow, Auntie Evie. I am going to make her regret that she ever met me.

Letter 15

Using My Free Will

Dear Auntie Evie,

I got up in the middle of the night while the lady was sleeping and then ripped up all the plastic bags that the lady put by the room where the car is. Was that ever fun. There is something about the feel of plastic that is so enticing. I then went back to bed rejoicing that I had some influence in my world. I slept like a puppy and felt quite good when I awakened. I then remembered what I did in a moment of sensory joy and decided to blame the plastic mess on Blimpy Bubble and Fart Face Amber. I am a master at blaming others, so I didn't have any difficulty. I raced over to the plastic bags and carried a few pieces and placed them in their beds. When the lady awakened, she saw the mess in their beds and realized what had happened.

Fortunately, the lady is not as smart as I am and was very upset with the pinheads. I must say that I am a super-smart dog. I really should take pity on the lady since she has limited thinking ability. Maybe she adopted me 'cause she felt that I could improve her intelligence and that people would think she was smart 'cause she was hanging out with a super-smart dog. I must try to be kind to her. I will let her pat me whenever she needs comfort. Life is strange, isn't it, Auntie Evie? All this time I was complaining how I hated the country and wanted to go back to the city. Now, I am not too sure. Maybe I should stay here for a while and continue my relationship with Sir Wellington. Then again, maybe I should return to the city before our relationship falls apart as they usually do. Actually, I think I'd better return. I can't let the lady drive the car by herself. I need to guide her and I would feel great remorse if anything awful happened to her. It's almost as if she is my puppy and I am protecting her. The poor lady, so alone in the world. I must take on the challenge of being a mother-like figure to her. I now understand that my purpose in life is to be her dog-mother. I could just cry with happiness. What a noble occupation for a noble dog. So you see, Auntie Evie, I am returning to the city so I can protect the lady and give her comfort, companionship and care. What a lucky, lucky lady to have me with her. Poor Sir Wellington. How sad he will be, but then again, I can always write letters to him and tell him about my days in the city. See you tomorrow, Auntie Evie, after my paws touch pavement and I say hello to a few puny trees!

Letter 16

Home at Last

Dear Sir Wellington,

We made it back to the city today and the lady took me to see Auntie Evie. What a happy reunion. She picked me up and I gave her a big lick on her face and she laughed and laughed. She didn't pay any attention to the two morons. How happy that made me. Auntie Evie knows that I am the Superior Dog. That's more than I can say for the lady. I quickly peed on a few New York City garbage piles to let all the dogs in the area know that Sice The Ice has returned

To tell you the truth, I wasn't quite sure that I would return. Driving with the lady is very scary and tummy upsetting. I sat beside her to navigate and the morons sat in their doggy bags in the back seat. *Ha Ha Ha,* no doggy bags for me. I am always in perfect control and never get emotional, like the lady. I tell you, we would have never made it back if it weren't for me. I made sure to bark at the other cars if they got in our way. The lady does nothing but look at the road. She is a totally boring person, but she is smart enough to know that she needs me to sit beside her and guide her. Sometimes, I try to take over the driving but she pushes me away. Then I ignore her and pretend to nap but all the time I am cursing her in my head.

Our relationship is very complicated. We managed to make it home without an accident, thanks to me but I wouldn't have minded if Fart Face and Blimpo got a bit shaken up, wouldn't mind at all. Wish the lady would leave them in the car and forget about them.

I tell you Sir Wellington, they don't belong in my line of vision. They do not have my DNA as you know. You and I have pure blood lines and we were meant for each other. We were born to find each other.

Unfortunately the lady needs my help and I have to take care of her. I know that's why I am living with her. I bring joy to her life. She is so lucky to have me. That's the reason I had to leave you but nothing else will stand in the way of our passion for each other.

I better sign-off now since I have to help the lady get to the apartment. She has to carry the morons 'cause they don't like elevators. They don't like to go outside either and prefer their wee wee pads. They are so immature and spoiled and they are ruining my life. When I get to the apartment I will wait in the kitchen to remind the lady that she has to feed me. I want to eat everything before the morons get to it, after all, I worked hard today. I will write tomorrow. Thinking of you.

Letter 17

Second Day in the City

Dear Sir Wellington

I awakened this morning in my own bed to the nasty sound of sirens. I missed that sound cause it always brings up my inner anger and fury'. Such nice emotions to have and express. The lady slept on her own bed but she didn't make it and I refuse to sleep on an unmade bed. I awakened before her and grabbed a few biscuits that I hid under my pillow. I am so smart, don't you think? The best way to hide biscuits is to sleep on them.

I had to wait a while for a walk since the lady was very tired. When will she get out of bed so I can be on my way. Of course, this is totally unfair to me since it is her responsibility to take me for a walk. I might have to use a wee wee pad. How insulting to do this to me. I want to pee outside and send messages to other dogs through the pee pee line. The lady and I will have to have a discussion about this. I can forgive her today since she at least made it to the apartment but no more forgiveness after this. Enough is enough. I can't let her forget that I am here. I had better get her up. I will try my howl of pain. That usually works. After all, it takes her time to use the bathroom and smear herself with creams. Luckily we don't have to do that. We stay good looking forever. I don't know who she is trying to impress. She doesn't have any boyfriends. Unless of course she is trying to attract a boyfriend. I suppose as long as she doesn't stink then there is hope for her. It's so much easier being a dog. We don't need creams and clothes. We walk around naked and smell each other's butts. She is finally finished and soon I will be on my way. Fart Face and Blimp are still sleeping. Glad I got to the wee wee pads first. Well I am on my way to find the best spots to pee in. I will take you for a tour if you ever visit. Then you can delight in the city's aromas. So glad it's not raining 'cause it's so difficult to find the interesting spots after the rain has washed them away, but we city dogs always find new spots and create a new pee pee line to send our messages. Will write tomorrow Sir Wellington. Got to retrain the lady on walking techniques cause its been two weeks since walking me in the city She has probably forgotten how to do it. Can't trust the human brain.

Letter 18

Getting Readjusted

Dear Sir Wellington

I have been meeting some old friends and a few new friends when I go outside. After all we are social animals. The lady has been taking me for walks but she is too controlling. I tried to bite a dopey looking dog's nose and she stopped me. That really pissed me off, since it would have been a big improvement to his face. Let's just say that not all dogs are good looking. I have been mostly very nice, I think, considering my superior rank. You know that I don't associate with the common variety or mixed breeds but sometimes they can be charming with training and guidance. When the lady took me to training school they said I was untrainable. That made me jump for joy cause they saw that I was superior and that no training was necessary for me. I see a lot of people who need training and guidance. Everyone, it seems, wants to pat me and that makes me want to vomit but I am too cultured to do that in front of them. I wait until I get upstairs to vomit. You need to understand that some people smell and some people have dirty hands. Don't they ever wash? I think they are trying to give me a disease. I growl at them to stay away and they think it's so cute. No matter what I do I can't seem to convince people that I don't want them around and the lady gets annoyed when I pretend to be vicious. I am only thinking of my health. I don't want to catch people's disease.

Aunt Evie visited me today. She brought me a squeaky toy for my collection. She also bought me a coat which is very upscale with my name on it. Aunt Evie is so psychic. How did she know that I wanted my own unique coat? Now I will look different from the morons as well as the morons outside. She took me for a long walk and everyone admired me. Now they can pat my coat and not me. How protected I feel. She took some pictures of me and will give them to the lady so she can send them to your lady.

I don't think she knows that I am in love with you since I keep my love life a secret. I don't want her to get jealous since she doesn't have a love life. It's not her fault since there are more dogs around with qualifications then there are human men. This <u>is</u> undeniable.

When Auntie Evie dropped me off at the front door I saw the lady talking to a handsome guy. I really didn't want to interfere but I was getting hungry and needed my dinner. So I barked at her, so she would notice me, but as fate would have it the handsome guy noticed me and it was love at first sight on his part, not mine. I am a very cool and controlled dog and even though I have many admirers I do not admire them back The bad news is, I think he admired me more than the lady. This is very sad for me cause I don't want to steal the lady's boyfriend. I am cursed with being beautiful and smart so that men and dogs can't help falling for me. I had better have my dinner before Fart Face and the Blimp get to the food first. I will write tomorrow.

Letter 19

Playing Matchmaker

Dear Sir Wellington,

I awakened cause there was a knock on the door. I barked back since I am the lady's protector. She went to the door, asked who it was and sure enough it was the sexy guy. I knew it would be difficult for him to stay away from me. He and the lady talked a bit. Then he took my leash and harness and said "come on Spice, let's go for a walk". I was very excited since I prefer to walk with him more than the lady who is very dull and has no understanding of the pee pee line and pulls me away from the garbage with its divine smell. Mr. Sexy let me stop at every garbage dump. He was very happy to be with me. I decided I would try to convince him to be the ladies boyfriend 'casue then he can be with both of us and take me for walks every morning so I won't have to wait for the lady to put on her creams. I will make a simple growl if he goes near Bubble the Blimp and Fart Face so he understands that he is only to communicate with me and the lady. He will get the idea. He is very intelligent for a human. When we returned to the apartment, I pushed the lady towards him by jumping on her and then on Mr. Sexy. I played very innocent and did a catch my tail circle dance to entertain them and waited for applause. I have to admit that I am very talented. They laughed together and then he left. I could feel the energy between them. I am sure he will return tomorrow. He is really a hunk. I bet he can do back kicks and run fast. I am going to take a nap 'cause I am exhausted. Matchmaking is difficult and I had the added burden of keeping the morons away 'cause they would only interfere. I am going to the ladies bed now.

I will have to arrange the covers and pillows so its suitable for me. I think my life is starting to improve since I am getting more control. Having power is one of the most thrilling things in the world and makes me want to get a pedicure I will write tomorrow. I think I am going to have a fun dream and visit the Doggie Planet.

Letter 20

Its Love Again

Dear Sir Wellington,

The sexy hunk showed up again in the morning. I knew he would 'cause he is in love with me. We went for a very long walk to a place that was fenced in and inside there were many dogs of all sizes and shapes. They were playing together and sniffing each other butts. Mr. sexy hunk took off my leash so I could run around also. It was heaven although most of the time I preferred to sit and watch. I even saw a dog that looked like you and we became friends. The sexy hunk was holding a bag of treats for me and I decided to share them to prove how well mannered I am. The other dogs were so happy. You never saw so many tails wagging. It was then that I started to realize that the sexy hunk was in love with me and admired my manners and good looks. I felt very joyful and special. I started to feel really sorry for the lady. It's ironic that she finally meets a sexy sensitive compassionate hunk and it turns out that he is in love with me. Of course that is understandable 'cause I am so special. My heart breaks for the lady but she can't compete with me. I wonder if I should run away with him? I think he will be coming to see me everyday. Too bad the lady is here. I have to tolerate it but she is improving. She is cooking for me and practically lets me take over her whole bed. Of course I have to re arrange the covers so they suit me. She even brings food for me and puts it on the bed so I will see it when I awaken. I wonder why she is being so nice to me? Maybe she realizes how much she loves me and that I won't to be here forever. You see Wellington, we don't live as long as people and there will be a time when we have to leave our adorable bodies behind and travel to the Doggy Planet where we originally came from. I know about this 'cause I dream about it every time I go to sleep. It's a lovely place. Lots of grass and trees and all the dogs playing around and eating good food. I saw many dogs there that I have known before and there are divine people who take care of us. They ask us to tell them when we want to go back to earth and get a new body and become puppies again. Some of us don't want to leave 'cause we are treated so well, but others decide to return 'cause they want to see their people again because their people are suffering and miss them so much. Don't tell anyone this Wellington, but I remember meeting you on the Doggy Planet before you decided to return to your lady and become a puppy again. I remember you from the Doggy Planet. We played together and that's why we are friends now. We will always meet our friends again on this earth planet since we always return to the people we love.

Sometimes our people come to visit us and we stay with them until we both decide to return to earth and meet again. It's really not complicated. We are and will always be with those who we loved and who loved us. It's sad in a way people don't understand that. I really enjoy being a puppy each time I return but next time I want to grow into a big dog so I can eat more food. It's so nice to be in charge which is the way it should be. So Dear Wellington, I will write again tomorrow, so we can continue our relationship. I have decided that I am going to be kind to my lady. She needs all the love she can get but I still have a lot of lessons to teach her. It's so nice to be in charge. The way it's meant to be. After all Dog spelled backwards is God. God with a loud Bark.

www.ingramcontent.com/pod-product-compliance
Lightning Source LLC
Chambersburg PA
CBHW052125110526
44592CB00013B/1755